CLOSE SHAVES

THE COMPLETE BOOK OF RAZOR FIGHTING

By Bradley J. Steiner

CLOSE SHAVES: The Complete Book Of Razor Fighting

© *1979 by Bradley J. Steiner*

Published by:

LOOMPANICS UNLIMITED
PO BOX 1197
PORT TOWNSEND, WA 98368

TABLE OF CONTENTS

SPECIAL NOTE TO THE READER

The instructions contained in this book are potentially *very* dangerous. The author and publisher do not recommend the careless study or use of the methods taught. Like all aspects of the COMBATO Self-Defense art, the science of razor fighting should be treated with respect and used only as a last resort under the threat of grave bodily injury or death at the hands of a violent criminal attacker.

Neither the author nor the publisher assumes any responsibility for injuries or damages of any type that result from a study of this book, or from the use of any of the methods described herein.

For information about the author's Self-Defense System and his various publications, write to him at the address below.

Bradley J. Steiner
Survival-Defense International
PO Box 9612
Phoenix, AZ 85068

INTRODUCTION

For a person living in modern times to turn to the use of primitive out-dated weapons for practical self-defense is ridiculous. Yet that is what tens of thousands of brainwashed devotees of "martial arts" systems have been doing for about two decades now in the United States, Canada, and throughout the Free World. This is thanks to the traditional "classical" instruction given by their various instructors, who by virtue of their expertise in martial arts ought to know better! These instructors probably *do* know better, in fact, but keep touting for their "nunchaku" (rice-flailing sticks!), "sai", "tonfa", long bo, etc., etc.,for the pure commercial gain it offers.

Now I'll not quarrel with any serious karate or kung fu teacher who teaches classical weapons for *art's* sake, and for exercise. So long as a teacher makes it clear to his students that it is in fact for *art* and for *fitness* -- and not for defense application in modern survival combat -- he is on legitimate ground. But beware of the "mystical expert" who stresses the use of Middle Ages para- phernalia when his students ask about practical modern defense in the street or in the home!

This is the age of firearms and nuclear warfare. We have long since passed sticks and stones as frontline weapons -- even if these sticks and stones are prettily-fashioned and sold for exhorbitant prices by martial arts supply houses.

Modern times have created modern needs, in close combat as in everything else. Most classical-oriented teachers are just draining the public's money, seeking every opportunity to exploit what is popular. By way of simple example: When my combat manual, THE TACTICAL SKILLS OF HAND-TO-HAND COMBAT (SELF-DEFENSE), first came out, it was immediatly received with hostility by so-called traditional instructors. One of these, who fancies himself a real master (with the "Zen mind" as one of his cohorts puts it!) hysterically and childishly attacked the book. However, the *non-classical*, more rational instructors (in the military, in various Federal and police agencies, etc.) received the manual very well, and it is now commonly used by serious combat instructors and students everywhere. In its second printing, the book is now recognized as a pioneer work in the field of hand-to-hand psychological and tactical-strategical studies.

Once my TACTICAL SKILLS manual started to gain in popularity among the defense-minded students and teachers, I received an order for a copy from one Oriental "kung fu expert" in California. This man read my book and then wrote a watered-down version of his own (carefully making sufficient changes to avoid a lawsuit for violation of the copyright law!) and now markets it widely. The manual he sells is practically useless, since he misses the most salient points of the subject, and the techniques he stresses are the nonsense classical kung-fu moves of his own traditional system (hardly anything new). My point is: He, despite all of his "devotion" to the art, is an ordinary money-grubber, motivated by hardly a shred of ethics or decency.

Don't look to the classicists and traditionalists for authentic, up-to-date instruction in survival combat! When it comes to *combat*, the most tactful thing I can say is: Forgive them for they know not of what they speak!

What I teach pupils of my self-defense system, COMBATO, is this: The art of bare-handed fighting is the art of *last resort* fighting. Before you go it barehanded against some empty-headed, drug-soaked, whacked-out psychopathic crapbag, *you use something against him!* In this regard, the best thing to use is a heavy caliber pistol.

Failing access to a good pistol, you use anything else that is at hand (e.g., a chair, lamp, stick, knife, bottle, book, etc.). A fighting knife (especially the proven Fairbairn and Sykes Commando model) is good if you don't have a gun, and most particularly if stupid gun laws like New York City's prevent the ownership of a handgun.

A short length of stick is pretty useful, provided you know how to use it properly. These are some of the types of handheld weapons I stress in COMBATO.

A straight razor is another practical modern handheld weapon, and its use is taught in my System to responsible pupils who have demonstrated no inclination to misuse such skill.

If the "ancient masters" had had a straight razor available to them, they'd doubtless have invented a "jitsu" (science) or "do" (way) for its proper combat employment. Since they didn't have straight razors, someone had to do the job of organizing a method of using it *today*. That's precisely what *I* did. That's what this book is all about. It teaches the basics of razor fighting that derive exclusively from my system of self-defense, COMBATO.

6

The material in this text is based on several things, practical experience being not the least. For almost 30 years I lived in New York City. I spent several of those years living in a ghetto-sewer where it was more risky to walk the streets than it would have been to go on patrol in Saigon during the Vietnam war. I couldn't carry a gun -- the murdering politicians have their anti-handgun laws, and thus insure that only criminals can safely carry firearms. I couldn't carry a stick -- it was too conspicuous and awkward in subways and crowds. Though I rarely carried anything (except sometimes a little razor), I survived the most dangerous neighborhoods of New York with but one small scar. Not too bad.

Today I earn my living by teaching -- via lessons, classes and books -- the art of survival under the worst possible conditions, to those who need these skills. *And I haven't lost a student to a mugger yet!*

I studied razor fighting because some pretty dangerous people were fond of carrying (and using) those damned insidious weapons. As I studied the art I got kind of fond of it, myself. After all, what's good for the goose... Anyway, the razor proved its merit to me, and so that *you* shall survive, I have written this book to teach the basic use of the straight razor.

Make no mistake about it, the razor has some very real *dis*advantages. One of them is that unless you're the right "type" of person, the weapon is useless in your hands. To be frank and blunt: You have to be able to move in fast on a man and slash a sharp blade of steel through his flesh. If feeling his warm blood (or *its* warm blood, the way *I* see it) spurt and spatter on your hands, and possible on your face and lips, bothers you, *don't* carry a straight razor as a personal arm.

The razor is not all that flexible as a manipulative weapon (like, for instance, the Fairbairn-Sykes fighting knife *is*). It does, however, give the *appearance* of being very fluid and manipulative when you're looking at it in the other guy's hand! However, as you will see in practice, there are really only a limited number of ways to inflict worthwhile damage with a razor. Remember, just because you draw some blood doesn't mean that the psycho is automatically going to drop on the spot.

The *physical* shock value of the razor is nil -- unless you have the good fortune to get a deep slash through the opponent's neck, throat or eye. Aside from that, the razor depends upon *psychological* shock for effect -- something that is considerable!

7

The razor's blade hacks and, unlike a hatchet that has weight and size, the razor's blade cannot really go too deep at all. Since that razor lacks a piercing point, it won't do to thrust it like a knife "through" the target. The heart, for example, is no target for a skilled razor fighter.

A razor is not the fastest weapon into action, either. Once in the hand, open, it can slash quickly enough in trained hands, but it is not faster into action than a gun or straight-blade fighting knife.

Because the razor is not really a killing weapon, it is desireable that the person who uses it be capable of physically following through any initial advantage a slash or two gains for him. He should be able to execute basic unarmed combat blows to augment and supplement his blade. When I teach razor usage as a supplementary weapon skill to a COMBATO pupil, I know the student *can* use hands and feet effectively -- but I mention this point here because I realize that this book will be read by some relatively inexperienced persons in the self-defense arts. GET SOME BASIC FIGHTING SKILLS!

I brought up the few disadvantages of razor use because I am fanatical about insuring that no student of mine should ever develop *false* confidence in himself, either in barehanded or in armed combat. KNOW YOUR LIMITATIONS, AND APPRECIATE THE ENEMY'S CAPABILITIES! Also, understand any weapon you use, and know exactly what it can and cannot be depended upon to do. These are the things that add up to victory in a fight for the trained combatant.

THE ADVANTAGES OF THE RAZOR

On the positive side there are *many* real advantages to the straight razor as a weapon. So, just as I pointed out the cons, let me here enumerate the pros:

1. The razor is very small, compact and handy. It takes up practically no space.

2. The razor is very lightweight. The problem of carrying it -- even for extended periods of time -- is really no problem at all.

3. With no pun intended, it must be noted that the razor gives its user an inestimable psychological *edge*. In any hand-to-hand fight, this would obtain. It is utterly blood-chilling to envision the possiblility of thin flashing steel in someone's hand slicing through one's body.

4. Razors are very inexpensive. You can buy a good one for less than half the price of a good fighting knife.

8

5. Razors are legally obtainable anywhere. Technically, they are not "weapons" at all, and you can even buy one in such restricted places as New York City.

6. A razor can inflict a terrifying wound and render an assailant paralyzed with utter fear, momentarily. In a fight, this is vitally important. Also, the fact that you appear "crazy" when you pull a razor is an advantage.

7. If a deep, clean gash suddenly appears on a man's arm, face, neck or leg, and uncontrollable profuse bleeding ensues, the opportunity to finish him off is presented easily, if he panics. Most people will panic if so wounded. Suddenly losing a lot of blood is not generally conducive to coolness and tranquility. A boot in the crotch or a knee-breaking kick can generally be delivered at such a point in the fight with no problem.

ATTITUDE, GUTS, AND FIGHTING SPIRIT

We need to get one fact absolutely clear: No person should *ever* carry *any* weapon that he is not thoroughly WILLING to use. "Willing" does not mean "able". I have known black belt level expert teachers who were *technically able* with weapons -- to the point of being artistically expert. But often they lacked the *will* -- the fighting instinct -- to *use* the weapons they had mastered against real people in real fights. Their mastery was plainly *academic*.

Be honest with yourself, please. If you really can't bring yourself to use a razor on someone, *don't carry one with you as a weapon*. It will only impede your actions if you're attacked, since while you are hesitating, the psycho will be pommeling (or possibly stabbing) your body into senselessness. Better to stick with your empty hands and *use* them, than carry any weapon and *not* use it, under actual attack.

If you are "willing" insofar as the use of the straight razor as a weapon is concerned, then you'll need only the guts and basic fighting spirit to use it.

"Guts" (i.e., intestinal fortitude) is partly inherent and partly manufactured through correct training. Training builds confidence and a confident man will give full reign to his inherent capabilities when pressed in an assault.

Civilization has dulled many of our animalistic impulses to survival -- but these impulses still remain dormant in all but the softest of us. Count on it: If you study and train well, the animal survival instincts *will* surface when the need arises.

9

If the reader will simply give himself over to the philosophy and techniques described in this text, he need have no fear of being ready when the moment of truth arrives.

Remember: Violent criminals and other trouble-making psychopaths should not be hysterically feared. They need to be realistically regarded as the potentially dangerous wild animals that they are -- and just like any wild animal when on the rampage, or when rabid, *these* two-legged specimens of depravity need to be *destroyed* when they threaten human life.

With an attitude such as the one I am trying to instill in you, *you*, and not the vicious dirtbag who assails you, will have the advantage!

Author is holding an actual straight razor (live blade!) that will be used to illustrate the method taught in this book. Note that the blade of the razor has been padded for protection... thus a real blade is used in training with no "real danger".

Author demonstrates that the padded blade is safe. With appropriate protective covering, even a razor's blade won't cause injury.

LESSON 1: CARRY, GRIP AND STANCE

Complexity is the hallmark of the impractical. The amount of money that the traditional karate, judo, etc. schools have been bilking the public for, *simply by offering endlessly drawn-out complicated courses in useless skills,* must be astoundling close to the National Budget.

Never, in any form of combative training, allow complex skills and stylistic variations to replace the *simple* basic moves. This applies resoundlingly to razor fighting.

For the purpose of the instruction in this Lesson, I shall treat carry, grip and stance as separate items; remember, however, that in use, these things blend together. No clearcut distinction is ever evident in application.

GENERAL POINTS

Make yourself used to holding and maneuvering your razor. Like any other weapon, the more you handle the razor, the more natural and comfortable and "right" it feels in your hands.

Do not think of your razor as any sort of "ultimate" weapon! *YOU* are the main weapon -- for without a fit, confident, trained body and mind, no weapon will avail you much.

Be practical. Don't get fancy and gadgety and start making "razor sheaths" and pouches and other idiotic toys. The razor can be practically carried in very unobvious natural places. The more you stick to this practical approach, the better off you will be.

Remember that a razor should come into play *only* when you mean to use it! A pistol might conceivably be used to hold a felon at bay or to "warn" him, merely by its presence. But a razor must never be used in this way. It is not a formidable enough weapon. It would be far better to splinter a man's knee and hack open the side of his neck, *then run,* than it would be to whip out a razor and "warn" some approaching crapbag that you'll not submit to his terroristic advances.

CARRY

The easiest place to carry your straight razor is in a side pocket. It should be deep enough to conceal the weapon. In the winter, keep your weapon in your outside *coat* pocket. Remember that if you need your weapon you will doubtless need it *immediately,* and groping for it just won't do!

Author feels that a simple pocket carry (above) is best for the straight razor. Note how easily and neatly the closed razor slips into the pocket.

With the razor concealed in the side pocket one may walk with his hand on the weapon and arouse no suspicion.

It is best to walk through any suspicious area with *your hand on your weapon*, fully ready to whip it into action on a split second's notice.

I have seen one custom-made shoulder holster for a razor, and with no desire to attack another's handiwork, I must say that I myself would not use such a device for a razor. The shoulder holster is excellent for a nice-sized straight-bladed knife, or for a handgun -- but this is because such weapons are *impractical* to carry in one's pocket! Why create problems? The closed razor is a delight to keep in one's pocket, since it is small, light, and easy to get to when there; so just stick to your pocket as the best basic place to carry your razor.

One other thing: The razor makes no bulge in the pocket, and one can very innocently slip one's hand into one's pocket *even when one's opponent is watching,* in most cases, and be able to suddenly bring the blade into action.

Facing a possible adversary, one may have one's hand on the razor -- ready -- and stand in an alert ready posture, without giving away the fact that one is armed.

I have known persons who carried their razors taped to a spot behind the neck (women often keep small knives under their hair). This is OK, I suppose, but it seems to me a little melodramatic. I never like keeping any weapon where I may expose myself to an attack while reaching for it. Reaching behind one's neck exposes one to a brutally effective kick or punch -- assuming one's adversary is mean and worthy (which I suggest you *do* assume!).

While many have used a behind-the-neck sheath, Mr. Steiner feels that when reaching for the weapon in this position, one leaves oneself too open. Note how a quick kick or punch could be driven into the razor-bearer's right side as he reaches for the weapon.

The pocket remains the quick, safe place to carry a razor.

There is only one way you will ever feel confident of your ability to get your weapon out and into action speedily: *by practicing!* By practicing you build real confidence and become physically adept at making movements that, in time, will be reflexive in an encounter. A weapon -- *any weapon* -- becomes a viable instrument only to the extent that it becomes an actual extension of your self -- of your will. Only familiarity and practice with a weapon can accomplish this aim.

Get used to having your weapon on your person, *ready.* THINK about its presence. FEEL it in your pocket often. This is the way to make carrying the razor a practical natural reality for you.

GRIP

The photos illustrate the best ways to grip the razor for hand-to-hand combat use.

When the razor is held with blade "locked out" it is capable of a very fast slashing attack, and the momentum generated by a properly executed swing will certainly deliver a telling blow. If you've got a quick, strong slash, you could really open up a man's face and hack through his neck or gash him severely almost anywhere with your attack.

This is the "lock-out" razor grip explained in the text.

The trouble with the locked-out grip is that it requires you to use your weapon in a manner that makes it possible for a semi-skilled opponent to fairly easily block your blow. If a low kick precedes your slash, no problem. But if you are relying on that one swipe to do sufficient harm so that you can escape (say, from a mugger) then perhaps the locked-out grip would not be the best choice.

The "fold-over" grips are outstanding, and in my opinion, the best way to go with a razor. They allow you to generate sufficient power behind your attack to deliver a possibly lethat blow-and-slash to the target. Against the neck, throat or eyes, such an attack will almost surely kill.

The thumb-side foldover grip.

Elaborate or fancy methods of holding the razor, beyond the three simple methods used in COMBATO are contraindicated. They are just too difficult to use instinctively in a fight. Stick with these *basic* grips, and practice getting your razor from your carry position out, and into one of the grips shown, *quickly*!

I stress again that these grips are designed to be used in combat! They are not intended for use in threatening or "warning" an obvious criminal dirtpile that you mean business. From these grips your basic attacks will be delivered with maximum power and

17

speed against an opponent. In the next Lesson you will actually learn how to slash and thrust, and where to do so, against the vulnerable razor-targets of your enemy's body. But first, get the simplest fundamentals down pat, and proceed from there. Before you know it everything will coalesce and you'll discover that you are confident and adept with your weapon.

The bottom-fist-side foldover grip.

STANCE

Forget the pretty karate and kung fu stances that you might have seen in various martial arts books, or in movies. While you're getting into one of those pretty positions, you could get killed. Just remember that the essentials of a good combat stance are:

- **Knees Flexed**
- **Groin Guarded With The Forward Leg**
- **Feet Neither Close Nor Widely Spaced**
- **Hands Where They Can Immediately Come Into Action**
- **Facing The Opponent**

All of the above battle-tested requirements can be met with a very simple stance, such as the one illustrated.

18

Above is the basic combat stance. Note that the razor is held in the foldover grip.

Such a stance should be assumed whenever you are confronted by an attacker, *and have sufficient time to ready yourself.* Often, however, circumstances will prevent the assumption of any stance.

I have always been of the opinion that stance is of rather negligible importance in practical combat. Most of the time the victim of an attack cannot assume any set stance. He must "go as is", so to speak, and spring instantly into counteroffensive action from whatever position he happens to be in when he is attacked.

For purposes of realistic training you should practice responding to assault from NO stance, as well as practicing your techniques from a combat-type stance.

From the standpoint of *attacking*, stance is a positive hinderance. When you yourself are initiating an attack, you want to employ the element of SURPRISE. Surprise requires that your approach "telegraph" nothing to the victim. Assuming a stance gives the whole thing away, and is never done in an effective attack.

In COMBATO I have a motto: "WHEN ATTACKED, *ATTACK!*" By this I mean that in my System I stress an *offensive* tactical approach to self-defense. Thus, when we find ourselves embroiled in sudden violence, we do ourselves *attack the attacker!*

Stance is not altogether usless, and I do in fact use a form of Kenpo-Ju-Jitsu stance in basic COMBATO drill and training. But stance, per se, must never become such an issue that we *need* some special stance before we can effectively function combatively. This would be anathema to survival.

Accept the basic stance shown as one that is as viable in combat as any stance can reasonably be, but don't become a prisoner to it. Learn to move and attack and defend from any normal position *as well as* fromn the combat stance, and you will be training right.

PROPER BODY MOVEMENT IN THE STANCE OR IN COMBAT

When you need to move -- whether in your stance (in practice or combat), or in any normal standing position -- there are a few principles that will aid you in speedy efficient movement, and maximize your combative ability. Above all, as regards footwork, remember the admonition to *never get fancy!* You can trip over your own feet or end up moving right into your enemy's Sunday punch if you get elaborate with your footwork.

The rules of proper footwork...

1. Get the idea into your head that your body must move as a *unit*, and always keep this in mind when you move.

2. Never cross your feet when moving or bodyshifting!

3. Always move the foot closest to where you want to go, *first*. The other foot follows.

4. Keep yourself balanced and poised as you move, always ready to attack or to defend on the instant.

COMBATO BODYSHIFTING DRILL

This is an exercise that I use in COMBATO to train students to move their bodies quickly -- as a unit -- in the main directions that they are likely to move. This is *not* intended for combat, only for training the student to quickly move and reposition his body with no wasted or awkward action. Try it. After a few days of daily practice you will enjoy a greater feeling of coordination and you will not have to "think" about how to move under pressure -- the right way will come naturally.

1. Ready position: standing comfortably, feet together.

2. Quickly shift left foot to 10 o'clock and let right foot speedily follow until both feet are confortably together.

3. Now shift right foot back to ready position and let left foot follow until feet are in the No. 1 ready position.

4. Shift right foot briskly to 2 o'clock and let left foot follow.

5. Shift left foot back to ready position and let right foot follow smartly.

6. Quickly sidestep left to 9 o'clock with the left foot and let the right foot follow.

7. With the right foot leading, shift back to ready position.

8. Shift quickly to 3 o'clock with the right foot leading, and let the left foot follow.

9. Shift back to ready position with left foot leading.

10. *Pivot* by turning counter-clockwise with the left foot stepping back and around to the right. You are now facing to the rear of where you faced in your original ready position.

11. Step back with left foot leading to the ready position.

12. *Pivot* by turning clockwise this time, doing the opposit of No. 10.

13. Opposite of No. 11 by using right foot to lead.

14. Briskly, from your ready position, step back to 8 o'clock with your left foot leading, allowing the right foot to follow.

15. With right foot, snap back to ready position.

16. Step to 4 o'clock with right foot leading and left following.

17. Return to ready position with left foot leading.

18. Take two fast, short and snappy steps back -- straight -- with either foot leading.

19. Return to ready position and repeat exercise two more times.

The above takes a long time to read, but all of the shifting will take you no more than 15 seconds, once you learn the steps. The exercise requires no fancy acrobatics. It is a straightforward and simple drill that anyone can learn to do and that will help anyone to achieve good footwork.

The relationship of the above drill to combat will become clear with practice.

Your carrying, grip and stance with your weapon constitute the bare bones beginning of combat training with the razor. You should review the points made in this Lesson several times and assimilate them well. It is too late to get the fundamentals straight when you're involved in a fight!

ON PHYSICAL TRAINING

The three broadest spheres of the COMBATO System are:

1. TECHNIQUES OF COMBAT
2. PSYCHOLOGICAL/MENTAL CONDITIONING
3. PHYSICAL TRAINING

As you can see, I attach *immense* importance to physical conditioning and training in my System! Under dangerous, confusing combat pressure and in the heat of a life-or-death fight *you must be in excellent shape, and you must have the raw power and muscular drive to make your techniques work!!* The old bromide "in the martial arts you don't need strength or muscle" is plain bullshit. Sure, if you're very, *very* highly skilled you may not need great strength, if you are up against an attacker who isn't totally out of his mind and if you are lucky, and if you manage to stop him quickly with a few fast well-placed attacks. But don't you think that's a lot of "if-ing"?

Even for women, in my Women's Survival-Defense Course, Lesson One is a physical toughening program for the girls to follow on their own!

Real fighting is dangerous, risky business. It has *nothing* to do with tournament karate, "sparring", or bouts in any polished "dojo" arena. You need: PHYSICAL CONDITIONING, MENTAL TRAINING, and GOOD, STRONG TECHNIQUES.

Insofar as using the razor is concerned, you will acquire your techniques and, I truly hope, your mental conditining, from studying this book. But you will need to do some actual physical training as a supplement to your practice, if your aim is to be totally equipped to meet any circumstance that might arise.

Since this is not a course in my physical training methods I am merely going to indicate some leads for you to follow up on, so that you can start a viable self-training regimen right away. If you'll invest this added effort you'll reap enormous rewards.

1. Weight Training.

The finest conditioning and strength development is done with weights. These exercises are especially recommended: *Squats, Presses, Dead Lifts, Curls, Bench Presses, Power Cleans, Rowing, Reverse Curls, Shrugs, and Snatches.* Use no more than three sets of any one exercise, and use no more than one basic exercise for each major body area. 5 to 8 reps per set are recommended. Train two or three times a week on alternate days, as a supplement to your practice. No workout should exceed 45 minutes.

2. Rope Skipping.

Recommended as a daily means of cardio-vascular conditioning, and to aid development of footwork. Running is a good alternative. Skip for two 3-minute periods per day, or run for 20 minutes, four times a week.

3. Calisthenics

Kneebends, squat thrusts, pushups, situps, legups, stationary running, twists, etc. all are useful and good to stay fit and tough. A session of 20 minutes a day with a balanced routine of calisthenics will keep anyone in shape, if weight training is unavailable.

4. Chinning, Rope Climbing, Swimming, Heavy Bag Punching, and Rowing.

All of the above are excellent additional exercises to stay in shape.

5. Punching Boards, Steel Bars, Etc.

The use of training aids such as punching boards, steel bars, etc. to harden the hands is also useful for the combat trainee. In COMBATO I employ steel bars for striking with the edge of the hand and buckets of wet sand or punching boards for hardening the fists.

Readers who are interested in more information on conditioning methods may contact me directly at the address in the front of this book, and I'll try to help out.

Okay, we're to advance. Let's proceed with the next Lesson in the art of razor combat.

LESSON 2:
VITAL TARGET AREAS AND THE BASIC ATTACKS

The purpose of a weapon is to amplify the degree of injury and damage -- and the efficiency of its delivery -- that you would otherwise inflict with your bare hands. A punch in the face is amplified by a bullet through the face; and a razor slash across the lips or eyes is a kind of middle-of-the-road attack between the punch and the bullet. The bullet is by far more efficient, but the razor generally is better than the fist.

The maximum efficient use of either bare hands or weapons is assured by directing attacks to *vital points*, rather than to general, pick-'em-as-you-swing targets. The best hand-to-hand fighters never waste time on ineffective targets; they go, like attack dogs, for the throat, etc.

The question of brutality is irrelevant. We are interested in survival; and often to survive we need to be brutal. If we are sane we do not pick fights. If we are reasonable we can see why we owe no ethics to those who assail us. WHEN ATTACKED, *ATTACK!* and be meaner, tougher, more ruthlessly cold and vicious than your attacker was! So much for "ethical consideration" and the squeamish souls who care about it.

It is safe to say that all of us would prefer *not* to be slashed anywhere with a razor. In fact, I would venture the premise that anyone, under normal everyday conditions, would be shocked and stunned even by a razor gash across his upper arm. However, we need to remember that serious fights bring their participants up to a kind of "super level" of stress and pain and shock tolerance -- especially the initiator of the fight, since he's the one who's best prepared. When this occurs, only an attack on a vital target will induce sufficient shock, pain or stunning effect to do any good.

It is enormously difficult to really stop a determined lunatic with a razor. But it *can* be done, provided one approaches the task by relying upon scientific attacks to critical "hit points".

Let us now analyze the best targets for your razor attacks...

VITAL TARGETS FOR RAZOR ATTACK

1. THROAT. This is one of the three possibly *fatal* targets for a razor attack, and I recommend initiating such an attack only when obvious and clear danger to your life or someone else's exists.

The entire area from the point directly under and back of the chin, right down to the hollow at the base of the larynx (Adam's apple) is easily vulnerable to a deep dig or gashing thrust of your razor.

Clearly, an opponent with any street savy will guard his throat well when he knows you have an edged weapon. However, this only means that:

a. The attack needs to be launched so quickly and with such utter surprise that virtually no chance exists for your opponent to block an attack at his throat; *or,*

b. A feint at the throat will cause the opponent to quite possibly *overreact,* and thus leave him wide open to a kick, punch, hand strike, toss of some object, etc.; *or,*

c. Your attack must be sufficiently brutal, fast and strong to smash aside his attempt to guard his throat.

Once a *deep* (not superficial) slash or dig of the blade has been made into the throat, it's all over for the opponent.

An attack to the throat. A fast, hard, accurate whipping slash here will end the fight!

And remember, the sheer TERROR of even a slight whipping razor slash at the throat that connects will surely enable you to dispose of any but the most professional and skilled fighter with relative ease. Ask yourself: What, this minute, does the thought of a gleaming razor blade chopping into your throat make you feel?

2. SIDES OF THE NECK. Also killing targets. The jugular vein and carotid arteries lie deep in the neck structure, but when a razor is held with the foldover type grip, and when a full-body power blow strikes the blade home, these dread targets *can* be hit. The blood and gore involved is a moot issue: How desparate are you? If it is you or him, opt for *your* survival, not his!

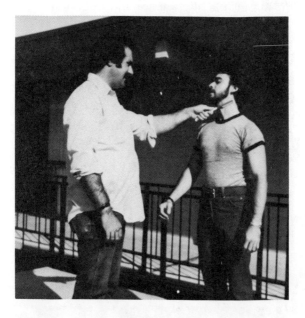

Probably the most gory attack -- ripping open the side of the neck.

The sides of the neck make somewhat easier targets to reach than the throat. However, never employ a "roundhouse" wild swing, since this can be easily blocked or avoided.

A HELPFUL TIP: Whenever the throat or sides of the neck are attacked with a razor, it helps to grab hold of the enemy's hair to stabilize his head for fairly easy cutting with the limited-thickness blade.

26

Also, *GROWL, GRIMACE, AND YELL!* Otherwise, you might remember that you are ripping a man's life out of his body, and you might hesitate.

3. EYES. A very hard, deep attack in the eye(s) can reach the brain. The best way for a razor to attack the eye is with *one of the sharpened, small corners of the end of the blade,* when the razor is held in the foldover grip. If you grab some hair (or an ear) and stabilize the head of your antagonist you can easily take his entire eye out of its socket.

Using the sharp corner of the blade and a foldover grip, the razor easily tears out the eye.

I cannot imagine a vigorous attack of this type which is followed by kicks to the agonized enemy's spine, kidneys and head not resulting in death. *USE ONLY IN LEGITIMATE COMBAT AND SURVIVAL SELF-DEFENSE SITUATIONS!* This stuff is not to be employed in a spat with your neighbor over a parking space.

27

4. INSIDE THE WRISTS. You might look at this as helping your enemy to commit suicide. Seriously, the exposed tendons and artery of the inside wrist area make it *very* highly susceptible to a razor slash. It is really doubtful that any but the most vigorous attack would kill by severing an artery, but it is just about the single most persuasive way I know to make some punk-scum release a grip he may have on you!

Though not as easy to sever the deepest-lying arteries as many believe, the inner wrist is terribly susceptible to a hard deep gash! Above, it is used to force an opponent to release a grip.

5. ACHILLES TENDON. A target that, when slashed or severed, will cripple instantly. This spot is somewhat unusual, except from a ground position. If you're floored and the enemy is not, grabbing his foot and ripping open his achilles will more than even the odds.

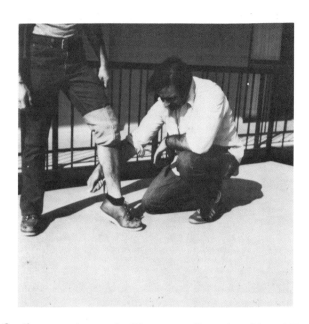

On the ground, armed with a razor, the vulnerable achilles tendon of the heel may be torn with a hard slash. VERY VULNERABLE!

6. GROIN. No, the razor is *not* practically employed to castrate. The groin is a highly vulnerable target on any male attacker. Ripping into the inner thighs (next to the crotch) and gashing any part of the groin area will at least distract the most savage adversary long enough to have a field day on his face.

7. FACE (GENERAL). In a situation where it's too dark (or things are happening too damn fast to single out a smaller target) be assured that *any* hard, vicious swipe into the enemy's face will do some respectable damage, and is almost guaranteed to distrace him for the kill.

8. EARS. A not-too-widely-known fact is that an ear can be most easily bitten, ripped or torn from the head with highly satisfying results in a fight. A razor corner driven hard *into* the ear *might* kill, but more likely would just cause unbearable pain and a serious injury. A razor that can be used with precision to hack off an ear is a razor that will terminate the fight for you.

29

How to attack the groin with the razor.

If you enjoy nit-picking, you can pick up three dozen martial arts books that list as many as three hundred so-called vital spots. In a fast-paced fight -- in *real* combat -- there is only a very limited number of practically usable targets. Only a real idiot with dulled reflexes and mongoloid stupidity is going to stand still and let you search out and pummel or slash his more minute vulnerable areas. Also, there is a real difference of opinion between what I find to be vital points and what some other "experts" claim are vulnerable targets. For instance, many judo and ju-jitsu teachers train their students to pinch a man's trapezious muscles (like Mr. Spock, on *STAR TREK*). In New York City I had several pupils (ex-boxers, street-hardened fighters, weight-lifters, dock-workers, etc.) who didn't give a hoot about all the pinching in the world! You could've placed a vice on their trapezious and they'd have laughed as they ripped your throat out. Also, using such stupid little "tricks" as grinding your knuckle into the back of an assailant's hand to make him let go -- *WHAT CRAP!* Try that on a *real* opponent some time!

Anyway... there are about 20 to at most 30 truly practical vital spots that make excellent targets in hand-to-hand fighting. For the razor, per se, I say this: MASTER your attacks against the eight targets I've indicated, and stick with *them*. Such an approach will lead in short order to really viable skill and *useful* knowledge.

By following the text and referring to the photos you will learn the most usable manuevers with your razor. *Don't* practice with a live opponent! Use your imagination to visualize an opponent. A partner was used by the writer in making the photos in this book merely in order to maximally clarify the manuever. If you wish to rehearse with a practice partner, *do not* use a razor. Either use a cardboard model (home-made) of a razor, or just pretend you've got a razor in your hand when you execute the moves. This will be more than sufficiently realistic to impart workable skill. I SAY AGAIN: NEVER, UNDER ANY CIRCUMSTANCES, USE A LIVE PARTNER TO PRACTICE RAZOR TECHNIQUES! This is stupid, risky, careless and for the purpose of acquiring skill, *totally unnecessary.*

BASIC ATTACK NUMBER 1: The lock-out whipping slash. This attack is executed with the razor held as explained in Lesson 1 for the lockout slash attack. Essentially, the best way to employ this attack is in a palm-down across-the-body whipping action (see photos below) to the eyes, neck, throat, etc. Power is *not* maximum with this manuever. Rather, the virtue of this attack is surprise and great speed. You can commence the attack with the razor totally hidden from your enemy and then, without warning, lash your blade out and chop him with it. Penetration, unless you are really strong and lucky, will probably not be too great. The blade just doesn't have the heft to go too deeply, and its limited size makes it impossible to drive it through the enemy without a very, very strong delivering the attack.

Practice first with no weapon until you make the attack with smooth maximum speed, and no "telegraphing" of your intentions. Later, start practicing with your razor. For this, a full-length mirror is useful. By watching yourself at first you will be able to see yourself as you will be visible to the opponent. You'll be able to cut away extraneous movement and unconscious "tip-off" gestures (like hunching the shoulders) that impede your effectiveness. Work for straight-line, simple movements, maximum speed, controlled force and the element of surprise in delivering your technique.

From an unassuming ready position, the combatant begins the lockout whipping slash.

Instantly! -- the razor whips forward gashing the opponent's throat in the completion of the lockout slash!

BASIC ATTACK NUMBER 2: Foldover grip attack (a). This attack is executed when the blade is folded back over the first finger (thumb side of the hand). There are three basic methods of delivery...

   (i) Inverted snapping slash.

(ii) Upward driving slash.

(iii) Outside-inward driving thrust.

Above is shown the inverted snapping slash (Basic Attack #2 (I).

The illustrations clearly depict the method of delivery for each of the three basic types of attack alluded to. Look at the photos carefully. *Study them.* Remember that the photos depict action that is "frozen" so to speak, and therefore you need to remind yourself when viewing the instructional plates that speed, *speed,* **speed, SPEED** is of the essence!!

The key to effective penetrative force in the inverted snapping slash is powerful tension of the chest and upper back muscles, and twisting the hips into the blow. The upward driving slash requires

33

stong forearms and biceps, as well as good back strength. The outside-inward driving thrust requires excellent tricep, shoulder, chest and back power for really sending the blade *through* the target!

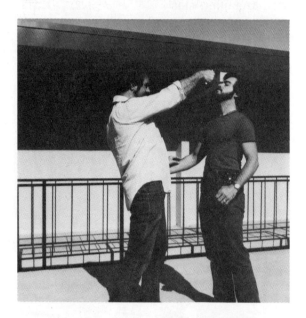

The upward driving slash (Basic Attack #2 (ii).

The outside-inward driving thrust (Basic Attack #2 (iii).

Facing a belligerent. Note how razor is concealed behind the leg in a foldover grip.

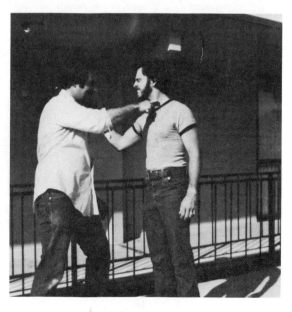

Immediately the attack is made! A direct gash into the neck.

35

BASIC ATTACK NUMBER 3: Foldover grip attack (b). This attack is delivered when the blade is folded over the pinky finger (edge of the hand) side of the hand (see illustrations).

I have found that I, personally, am capable of delivering my most powerful attacks when the razor is held in this position. And, remember, power *is* vitally important, to compensate for the razor's inherent weakness of lack of both size and heft.

One of my favorite attacks is to grab the enemy's ear or hair with one hand and whip in a downward smashing bottom-fist blow right across his neck/facial area with the opposite (razor-holding) hand (see photos). This is the old bottom-fist hand-to-hand attack -- modified to incorporate the razor!

Another use of the blade when held like above is to rip open the enemy's grabbing wrist, when he attempts to seize your wrist, or your clothes (see photo).

A palm-down whipping drive directly ahead into the opponent's eyes or face is a natural for this grip. Works well and is very effective!

A variation of the foldover grip and another way to face a person without betraying that you are holding a razor. From this position an attack can...

...follow at once! This time the neck is ripped open by a reverse type of gash.

NOTE: I have seen the razor employed with this grip in a manner roughly similar to brass knuckles in that the razor was used to augment the effectiveness of one's punch. That such an attack can be formidable, I do not dispute, but I ask you to remember that such a direct-punching attack is generally easier for the opponent to avert or block than the more unconventional techniques I have indicated.

Practice the methods explained over and over, incorporating this drill with practical carry, grip, stance, etc. And please do not allow yourself to become smug once you have mastered these moves, and start improvising more acrobatic ones! Just master the moves given. They are the ones to be relied upon in a fight.

Use your imagination to consider the endless possible applications of these simple attacks under all of the possible situations that could occur. Consider the application when you are seated; when you turn around to face someone behind you, when it is dark out, etc., etc.

The best way is the *simple* way! Paractice the moves in this Lesson for a few days before moving on to Lesson 3.

LESSON 3: STRATEGIES AND TACTICS

There is much more to successful and effective fighting (with or without weapons) than *techniques*. Tactics -- or the way we use techniques -- are essential to success in combat. Good tactics and sound strategy can tip the scales in your favor, even when you are "outgunned", so to speak. A larger, stronger, or better armed opponent than yourself is not always or necesarily guaranteed victory in an encounter with you, *provided* your mental equipment and methods of handling yourself and your weapon are up to snuff.

In this Lesson we will examine some of the essential tactics and strategies of hand-to-hand combat. Specifically, we will emphasize those that are most useful to you when you are armed with a razor, and that will, *if you master and apply them*, put you ten steps ahead of the average street punk.

What is imperative is that you continually bear in mind the relationship between tactics and strategy and your actual physical skills. One does not replace the other, ever. The value of these aspects of your training is reciprocal. Strategy and tactics make techniques maximally effective; and techniques properly learned and mastered make tactics and strategy your staunch ally.

Re-read this Lesson several times and think about how everything you will be taught applies to what you have learned previously -- and to what you have yet to learn, as you get there in your course.

FEINTING

To "feint" simply means to make your opponent believe that you intend to make a certain move, or deliver a certain type of attack, and then *not carry your gesture through*. Instead of actually making the move you led your opponent to believe you were going to make, *you use whatever position your opponent placed himself in* when reacting to your feint, in order to execute a decisive attack against him.

A successful feint can leave an opponent wide open to a fast, powerful attact -- an attack that *ends* the fight.

Any time you have a weapon held so that your opponent can see it, *he will automatically assume that you intend to use it, and that you will indeed attack with that particular weapon*. REMEMBER THIS POINT!

One would generally assume that feinting for the razor-wielder would involve a gesture, say with the *free* hand, so that the razor could do its job swiftly and cleanly, right?

Wrong.

Feinting, remember, is *deception*. I stress using the *razor* to feint, and then, for example, delivering a nice, hard kick to the knee or groin, when the opponent "covers up" to guard against the razor. Then, after you've struck your first blow where the enemy never thought you would -- and you've thus disconcerted him -- you go full steam ahead with your blade!

Example of a feint to the face with the razor.

Count on it: An opponent will surely feel you "mean it" when you feint with a razor! Could he afford to think otherwise?

Naturally, more conventional feints could be used, with the free hand, for instance. But generally the feinting approach with the weapon works best.

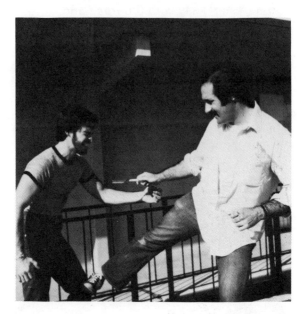

A side kick into the knee, immediately following the feint in the previous photo.

THROWING SAND, DIRT, OR GRAVEL

When I lived in New York City I always carried a handful of gravel (purchased for 15¢ at a pet shop) in my coat pocket. A bladed weapon was invariably in my *other* pocket. The purpose was to give me a pretty efficient one-two combination in case I needed it: First, a fast toss of the gravel into an opponent's face; Second, an instant follow-up with my bladed weapon!

Throwing sand, dirt, keys, small change, gravel, or *anything* suddenly into a person's face will give you eons in which to finish him off at your leisure! In a restaurant, remember the pepper shaker! Unscrew it and dump the contents in your hand and you can disconcert two or three attackers in one fell swoop!

Tossing sand or dirt (or even pepper!) into the eyes of your opponent to distract him momentarily.

When opponent covers his face as dirt is thrown, slash at his neck or throat!

41

USING HAND AND FOOT BLOWS IN CONJUNCTION WITH YOUR RAZOR

Never allow yourself to become dependent upon any weapon to the point where you feel helpless without it. *You* are your primary weapon. Develop sufficient skill in punching, clawing, kicking, butting, stomping and general hand-to-hand so that you are formidable bare-handed. *Then* add your weapon skills!

Remember always that just because you're armed with a razor, (or any other weapon, for that matter!) there's no law saying you can't spit in your opponent's face, kick his groin, or elbow him in the teeth. Your weapon must be an extension of yourself, and *you*, yourself, must go into any fight totally, using kicks, gouges, etc., *along with your weapon*, to insure victory.

You will, if you ever need to save your life with a razor, be in a desperate do-or-die situation. In such an instance do not sell your body short as an all-inclusive weapon, and think solely of applying your razor. You may overlook the chance to deliver a kick that could send your enemy sprawling.

And lastly, remember: Once the enemy crumples or falls, *don't join him on the ground!* Bring him down with your weapon, by all means, if that's possible... but finish the job with your *feet!* Or, if in your home, use a chair or heavy lamp or fireplace poker on him when he's down. But don't go to the ground with the opponent!

USE OF SURROUNDING AREA

A chair can be thrown into an oncoming opponent's legs. A wall can guard your back. Rocks or dirt can be picked up and thrown. We could go on endlessly. The point is: Wherever you happen to be when the action starts, *make your surroundings serve you!*

A pupil of mine who was assaulted indoors was able to obtain a grip on his attacker's wrist. He suddenly whipped the attacker's hand sideways, right into the corner of a heavy piece of furniture. This caused a moment's distraction, and my student's fists and feet terminated the encounter.

Make your surroundings serve you in a hand-to-hand fight.

Probably the best way to train yourself to implement the above idea is to constantly *think* about how various elements of your surroundings, at any given time, and in any given place, could be used to assist you in a fight, should one occur. By thinking along these lines you will be amazed at how "always prepared" you are and feel, regardless of where you may be.

Yelling should come automatic to you in a serious fight. Suddenly, with no warning, turn crazy! Grimace like a rabid madman and scream in as murderous and blood-chilling a manner as you can. Combine this with your attack, and the opponent will probably not even *see* the razor before it rips him open!

Yelling serves to tense your important leg and abdominal muscles, to startle and "freeze" the opponent for a split second, and to render your mind hell-bent on aggressive action. It distracts you from the brutal nature of what you're doing, and lets you block out your own ruthless assault from your total sensitive-awareness.

Just *yelling*, by itself, can totally unnerve an untrained or relatively inexperienced opponent, when done by an expert. The true kiai shout can be so piercing that the assailant's mind totally loses its ability (for several seconds or more) to give and activate "commands" to the assailant's body! Thus, an opponent who had everything set in his mind before he attacked you could conceivably be stunned into momentary senslessness if a blood-curdling yell suddenly shocks his mind. At that instant, he's yours. You can rip into him and dispose of him with ease.

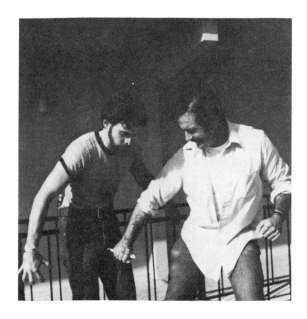

Held as a yawara stick (closed) the razor may be used to effectively jab the groin...

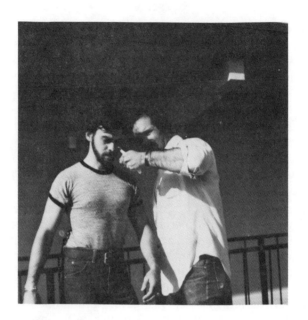

...or the eye!

CLOSED RAZORS

A straight razor can be an effective weapon even when closed. By holding it securely (see photo) it becomes a potent "yawara stick" type of weapon, and with fast powerful delivery, it can penetrate the base of the throat, the temple, the solar plexus, or punish a kidney! Driven into the groin, such an improvised yawara stick will prove most disconcerting for your tormentor.

If you need a second or two to get your razor open and into action, its use initially as a yawara stick could give you the chance you need.

REVIEW OF GENERAL TACTICS AND STRATEGIES

I never tire of saying that self-defense is *war in microcosm.* View it as such, and attach the same importance to your strategy and tactics that a general attaches to his army's. These, in a nutshell, are the nitty-gritty things you'll want to burn into your brain...

1. Yell!

2. Grimace like a lunatic!

44

3. **Be aggressive and wild!**

4. **Use the element of surprise!**

5. **Throw something in the enemy's face to distract!**

6. **Use all of your available mental and physical power!**

7. **Use anything in your surrounding area to assist you!**

8. **Always kick low to disconcert!**

Now, with our initial ground covered, we are ready to proceed to the nuts and bolts aspect of our study: *actual examples of how you can apply and employ your razor as a viable weapon of self-defense against a violent, dangerous criminal attakcer.* In the next Lesson we shall see how your razor can be instantly brought into play against a mugger, street-fighter, or other serious determined assailant. Make absolutely certain that you've assimilated the material in Lessons 1 through 3 -- then go right on to Lesson 4!

LESSON 4:

SELF-DEFENSE TECHNIQUES WITH THE RAZOR

Once the pupil has assimilated the basics of grip, stance, fundamental attacks, vital points and tactics, etc., it is time to proceed with actual study of technique application -- that is, with self-defense situations and appropriate razor fighting responses.

Let us commence by viewing self-defense responses realistically, and by understanding their proper function in preparing the student to fight hand-to-hand.

Traditionally, the arts of aikido, ju-jitsu, and certain of the karate styles have stressed the approach of learning "one defense for each attack variation". The result of this approach has been to develop self-defense methods employing as many as three to four *thousand*(!) individual, specific techniques! Obviously, such an approach to the study of self-defense is very, very time consuming. Also, I frankly question its need or its practicality -- even if one is prepared to invest the required time in study.

In COMBATO I developed a method of *reducing* the quantity of specific techniques, but employing tremendously-forceful and all-encompasssing *combat combinations* that have virtually unlimited applications. They are *generally applicable* movement/technique combinations that when learned will offer their master endless variations which his practice will enable him to make easily "on the spot" when required, UNDER COMBAT CONDITIONS! Followup in all of my defense-attack methods is enormous. In fact, my motto of WHEN ATTACKED, *ATTACK!* is implemented to the point of overkill. But in a crisis, one can never be "over-gunned".

What happens, in effect, when a COMBATO pupil is attacked, is that the attacker -- with his first initial aggressive movement -- triggers a perpetual, overwhelming and unending barrage-like counteroffensive that the COMBATO pupil executes without physical or mental reserve. The COMBATO man goes "all-out" and he does so *instantly*. There is but a split second elapsed before brutally effective attacks are raining down upon the assailant. Once so triggered by his attacker the COMBATO man becomes a wild animal and proceeds to continue his counterattack until every vestige of danger to himself or to his loved ones has been neutralized. "Comealong" grips, mild trips, simple releases are *never* used. Not because I am especially brutal or because the

COMBATO pupil is trained to be especially mean (remember: the COMBATO man is the *defender*; he did not start the fight), but because there is no rational justification for the victim of any attack to incur greater risk or danger to himself than is absolutely necessary. And there is no way to foretell the exact intent of some garbage heap who lays a hand upon you. Many murders have been initiated by a lapel or wrist grab; and rape has often been the outcome of a"harmless" embrace. The self-defense pupil takes no chances. *Survival* is his aim and purpose and his only concern. *His* survival, and the survival and safety of his loved ones -- AND THAT'S THAT. Period. One who raises his hand aggressively or menacingly to another *deserves anything his victim can or chooses to do to him.* The violent crimninal who is killed during commission of his act should be written off with the public waste that our communities incinerate in garbage dumps. There is hardly any need or reason to care about him.

The concept of all-inclusive defense applies essentially to razor work. One "trick" is never the answer to a critical defense emergency. Anyone who believes that it is has much to learn.

When you study the movements described, bear in mind that these are representative examples of what you can effectively do in a fight; they are not rigid, absolutistic "only ways" of using your razor.

Study these few representative defenses well -- but, more importantly, study the *concepts* that underlie their application. Learn to think -- and fight -- in this manner. The whole approach is ATTACK WHEN ATTACKED! If you think of your body and mind as a reflexively-reactive weapon, triggered into action by your assailant's approach, you will have learned the most essential fact about responding -- with or without a razor in your hand -- to any attack.

IF YOU ARE EXPECTING TROUBLE, YOUR RAZOR SHOULD BE OUT AND READY FOR USE!

REPRESENTATIVE DEFENSES

1. DEFENSE VS. A LAPEL GRAB (a)

This is a very common form of assault, and it is a very, very common *initial contact* move, after which a more serious attack is followed. Look carefully at the photos illustrating the correct procedures for defense when your lapel has been seized.

Response to a lapel grab attack. At opponent's grip, you are ready with your razor...

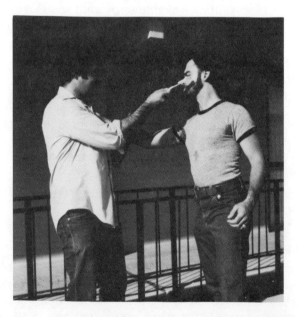

With your left hand (above) block his gripping arm outward to distract him from a simultaneous fast whipping slash across his eye.

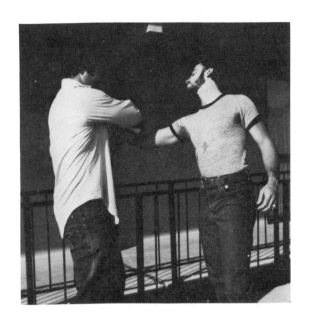

Your slash follows through, right across the enemy's face, hopefully taking a portion of his eye with it.

Now whip the blade back, across his face in the direction opposite to the first slash. Follow through with your entire body...

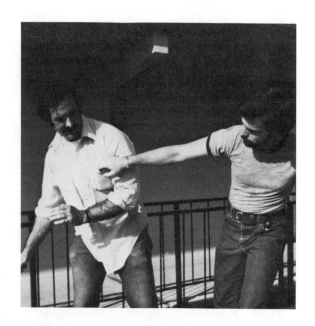

...bringing you into the position above.

And quickly return your body with a hard pivot, as you whip the blade into the opponent's throat!

These pictures show more than words can describe, and all that can be said in further clarification of what needs to be done is: Move with lightning speed. Use all of your available physical power and mental concentration. Yell. Be utterly ruthless, and follow up. The movements of your defensive response as illustrated represent only the *start* of your total defense. To be effective in a real street situation, it is necessary that you propel yourself into continually following up on the attacks you make.

Another lapel grab defense.

Whip the blade down hard, gashing open the enemy's wrist.

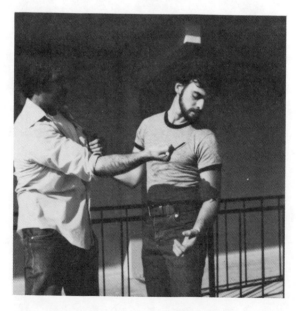

Quickly snap your blade up and across his face or neck as the slash attack to his wrist draws his attention.

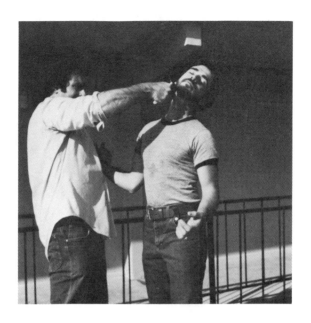

And rip him again with another hard slash to the face or neck!
BE FAST!

2. DEFENSE VS. A LAPEL GRAB (b)

This is a variation attack, in which your assailant employs both arms to grab you, instead of only one. In actuality, you are safer in this position, since the opponent has succeeded in tying up both his hands instead of one, and he has -- by seizing you -- stabilized your balance and assured a predictable distance between you for your counterattack.

53

A gutter rat grabs you with two hands -- "tough guy" style.

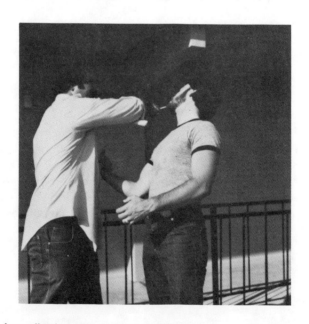

Immediately swipe right over and across his arms, tearing open his face or eyes.

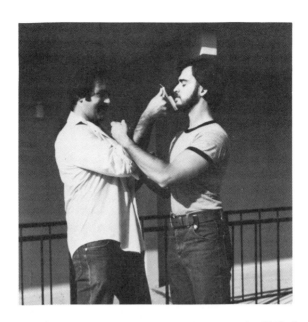

Alternate move: Go right up between his arms and split his lips and nose with a vicious slash!

A hard knee blow into the crotch is a fine followup after the first slash or two has started the blood running!

3. DEFENSE VS. A PUNCHING ATTACK

The key here is to avert the initial attempt that the assailant makes to punch you, and close the gap, tying him up momentarily so that you can go to work on his flesh with your blade. The razor is useless at a distance, so *as soon as you've avoided the punch*, get in there fast and cut him up!

Some punk decides to punch your face in.

Deftly dodge to the outside of the punch, parrying his blow harmlessly aside, and...

...Whammo! Snap your blade home! A quick ripping slash into the opponent's eye or face will give him second thoughts about starting fights!

Controlling the arm you parried, follow up with a second slash, this time at the bastard's neck.

Now, draw back and whip a third slash across his exposed face or neck.

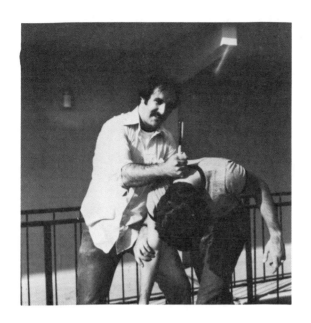

And complete the defense by smashing the end of the razor (yawara stick style) down across his neck.

4. DEFENSE WHEN YOUR PATH IS BLOCKED IN THE STREET

The law says that you are allowed to use only enough force to defend yourself, and *only* when an actual attack has materialized -- so the idea of responding with violence prior to an actual physical action from the opponent may conflict with the law. I DO NOT ADVOCATE BREAKING ANY LAWS. ALWAYS BE A GOOD CITIZEN AND OBEY THE LAW. For informational purposes only, then, I present this sure way to remove some filthpot from your path when, belligerently, and obviously intending to do you harm, he blocks it.

Some street hoodlum blocks your path with obvious violent intentions.

But surprise! The scumbag discovers that he's picked the wrong victim! You smash your free hand quickly into his nose to distract.

Then drive a powerful blow with your blade right up into his groin, driving your BODY into the blow for p-o-w-e-r!

Slash his entire body right up the middle, and finish by tearing open his neck and face -- or by coming as close to that ideal as possible!

And terminate the human mistake with a knee driven into his groin.

5. DEFENSE WHEN A PUNK ATTEMPTS TO PUSH OR SHOVE YOU

Situations where this general form of attack occurs are very similar to situations where one's path is blocked (See Defense No. 4, above). The scumbag wants to terrorize you a bit before assailing you. By following the defensive procedures indicated in the illustrated sequence above, you can carve a nice message in the dirtbag with little danger to yourself. But be sure to *act fast!*

CONCLUSION

Since actual hand-to-hand combat is an endlessly fluid, and never static, process, the representative examples of defenses in this Lesson are to be taken only as *suggestions of possible responses* when and if you are ever actually under attack. Do not hesitate to improvise upon, modify or alter these defenses to suit yourself. Just don't get acrobatic, cute or fancy, and thus destroy the practicality of the method itself.

Also remember this: from the simple basis given in this Lesson and from the material expounded in the preceeding three Lessons, a literally endless variety of specific defense combinations can be made up. It all depends on you.

With the basics of grip, stance, strategy and movement mastered -- and with the theory of defensive attack understood, there is no limit to how far one can go in developing further.

LESSON5:
SELF-DEFENSE *AGAINST* THE RAZOR

Effective defense against a skilled razor attack is most difficult, if not impossible; but this is *not* because the razor is so terribly formidable in itself. Rather, it is because an assailant needs to take you totally by surprise (or he needs to "psyche you out") and if he succeeds in doing that he can finish you even if he's unarmed.

Defense against a razor fighter who fails to catch you by surprise is *far* from impossible; and if you've got your wits about you and if you go at him like a rabid dog, *you will win the fight.*

I want to reduce this Lesson to the fundamentals and essentials, and I want to give you practical usable material that you can stake your life on. So I'm not going to pad this lesson with ridiculously complicated, intricate, acrobatic movements that make for great exhibitions but leave you wide open in a serious *real* fight. If you study, learn and *practice* the moves and suggested tactics in this Lesson you will stand at least a 90% chance of success against a razor wielding assailant -- provided you see the attack coming. I know of no way to assure a 100% chance of victory in anything, and I maintain that anyone who claims to be in possession of such knowledge is either a fool or a liar -- or both.

ALERTNESS

There is little chance of successful defense against anything if you are caught totally unprepared, in a relaxed mental and physical state. Therefore, *alertness to danger* and to the possibility of attack is in this, as in every instance, your frontline defensive tactic.

If we wish to be technical we can assert with some degree of truth that an attack against you by a razor-bearing opponent can occur anywhere and at any time. This is *technically* true, but practically ridiculous -- and you know it. You are *not* in the same degree of danger regardless of where you are and regardless of whom you are with.

What you need to cultivate is the habit of *regulating your levels of readiness depending upon where you are and upon who and what is around you.* In other words, when you are sitting at home watching TV you can (except in the very rarest of exceptional instances) relax and assume a mental-physical posture different from one you would assume walking through a ghetto neighborhood at half past two on a Friday night.

THINK. Whenever you leave your home you should "raise" your mental level of readiness for trouble. This is neither foolish nor paranoid. It is practical, sensible and realistic -- as any mugging victim or rape victim can assure you, provided he or she has lived through the experience.

In most instances where an attack against a person succeeds, it does so because the victim IS NOT PREPARED FOR TROUBLE. *In every single instance where a combat-trained person is successfully assaulted this is true.* BE PREPARED.

Whenever you are not clearly in a safe, secure place and among friends, you should be alert to the possibility (if not the liklihood, as you would be in a bad neighborhood) of an attack.

In COMBATO I stress, stress again, and *stress again*, this all-pervasive need for alertness at all times. This is not the sort of thing sproting combat and tournaments teach a person -- for one who "plays" at different combat forms actually defuses his own defense mechanism to a degree. He learns to be ready "on the mat" or "in the arena", but to relax when the match is over. In COMBATO training, the opposite occurs. A pupil is taught to relax and *learn*, and then to *be alert to danger*, when he's "on his own"! No one is in danger in a self-defense school (unless the class is being conducted by a moron for the benefit of idiots). Danger exists outside -- in the street.

BE ALERT AT ALL TIMES, AND LET NO ONE COME NEAR YOU UNLESS YOU KNOW WHO THEY ARE AND WHAT THEY WANT.

When you're walking down the street keep your hands *out* where they can do you some good in averting a sudden attack. If it's raining or snowing, too bad. Don't walk near parked cars or near buildings in the street. Human pestilence enjoys lurking in the shadows for victims who approach unawares within arm's reach. Again, if it's inclement weather, tough. Get wet -- but don't get killed.

If the reader will always make a habit of this *alertness* that I am stressing so much, he will have reduced the altent efficiency of any possible attacker by at least 60%. In many instances an attacker will be deterred *merely by a show of readiness on the part of his*

65

intended victim. Remember: the scum is not looking for a match or a contest. The scum wants a *victim.* Anyone who does not appear to be easy pickings encourages the criminal vermin to step wide and look elsewhere for a target.

Your demeanor, your step, your bearing and posture all have a great deal to do with alertness and readiness. Walk briskly, confidently and assuredly. Keep your eyes open, your head up, and look around as you walk, being alert to even the slightest noise near you or behind you, and making full use of your peripheral vision.

A man who appears thus is not projecting the message, "I'm afraid; I hope to God nothing happens to me!" He is projecting the message, "I'm here and I'm alert and I know where I'm headed, and I'm going to get there, *regardless!*" This is not what the scum wants to attack.

WHENEVER POSSIBLE BE ARMED

It is no secret that I am pro-gun and a real firearms LOVER (not a gun "nut", but a gun *lover!*). I love anything that can make a crippled old woman the equal of two hulking, muscular crapbags who would rob and beat her. I love anything that lets a decent man protect his home, his woman and his children from the dreg-muck filth that would victimize them. I love MIGHT in the hands of the RIGHT. And to the unthinking idiots who say, "But criminals also can use might -- and can get guns!", I answer, *"GUNS HAVE ALWAYS BEEN TOTALLY AVAILABLE TO CRIMINALS AND THEY ALWAYS WILL BE. THAT IS WHY THEY MUST ALWAYS BE MORE AVAILABLE TO THEIR POTENTIAL VICTIMS!"*

In any case, I urge anyone who can to obtain, and learn the proper combative use of, guns. If you live somewhere like New York City, where only criminals can get guns but not decent citizens, I am sorry for you, but let's work with what we can, eh?

Carry some gravel or sand in your pocket and at the first sign of aggression from some cockroach, toss it in his face. An umbrella (with the metal tip filed to a point, as I always teach my lady pupils!) is a dandy weapon. Almost anything at all may be used simply to distract an opponent by throwing it in his face. *Remember this!*

The razor is not a stabbing implement, it is exclusively used to slash. The opponent must get real close. So, a moment's delay in his advance caused by yur suddenly throwing something in his face will give you the second you need to kick him into senselessness.

66

Unquestionably, absolutely, invariably and indisputably, *kicking* is your best and most effective defense against a razor-wielding assailant. Blocks with your arms are sometimes useful, to be sure. Even spitting might give you some moment's advantage. But good, fast kicks delivered mercilessly into the enemy's vulnerable body areas constitute the single best and most reliable defense measu;re against a razor (or a knife, for that matter).

If he slashes at your leg when you kick (assuming you kick in a slow unskillful manner) you'll not suffer much for it. The razor's slash -- if your trousers don't take the brunt of it -- will not even be felt until after the fight. The wound won't be serious. In fact, your worst danger from kicking would be the chance of having your leg grabbed. And this can be avoided by: *a)* Kicking properly; and *b)* Kicking LOW.

HOW TO USE YOUR FEET AGAINST A RAZOR ATTACK

Kicking high is OUT. Don't attempt kicks above your attacker's groin -- unless you like the prospect of losing the fight. High kicks look fantastic and that's why they are used in the movies, in martial arts books, and in demonstrations. But low kicks save lives, win fights, and *work* when you need 'em! *Kick low.*

Your basic target is the TRIANGLE. This is formed by your attacker's groin and knees (the three "points" that form the triangle). No matter how your attacker holds himself or how he comes at you, *at least one* (and generally two) points of the triangle will be exposed to you. THAT'S YOUR TARGET! Break the bastard's legs or kick his testicles with all your might and you will slow his advance forthwith!

The side thrusting kick is the best way to deliver your foot attack to the advancing razor-wielder. This excellent kick is delivered as follows: Shift either foot back, to your rear, and throw your body weight on *it*. Draw your arms up as you shift to guard your face and body and turn, doubling over slightly for solid balance. You've now brought your torso completely out of harm's way and the worst that your opponent can do is cut your arm or tear your shirt with his weapon. Draw your leg (the one nearest the opponent) up and bring your knee toward your stomach. The edge or bottom of your kicking leg now faces your adversary. Suddenly lash out hard, thrusting your entire hip and side into a brutally powerful kick, aiming to go *through* the target you attack. Lash out and snap back after contact. REPEAT THE KICK!

67

The start of the basic side kick -- combat style.

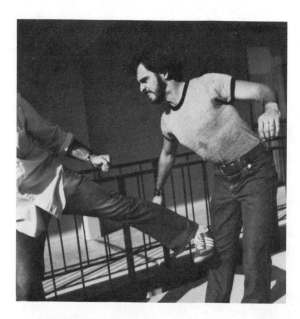

The completed kick -- right through the knee! Thrust hip into blow and drive heel forward.

68

The value of this defense is so great that I cannot overstress the need to master it thoroughly. *If you learned no other tactic of unarmed combat,* your mastery of this kick would assure victory in 80% of the face-to-face fights you would ever be likely to encounter. One student of mine in New York City (the Bronx, to be exact) floored *two grown men* by deftly and ruthlessly applying the side kick against them when they cornered her. She was 14 years old, and they were adults. Yet the incredible power of this kick, even from a child, and the extreme vulnerability of the targets made the defense amazingly efficient. Only 75 pounds of counter-joint force will break a knee, and even a 14 year old girl, weighing 90 to 100 pounds can deliver twice that, easily, *with practice.* Imagine what *you* can do!

Should you be standing with one side completely or partially facing the opponent already when he moves in, *just kick from there*, avoiding any unnecessary footwork and merely shifting your weight to the foot farthest from the assailant.

The front kick is sometimes viable against a razor-wielder, but the side kick is far better. Best use of the front kick is when the opponent, facing you, *reaches* for or starts to pull out, a weapon. Then just let fly with a super-fast ball-of-the-foot snap kick right into his testicles, and whip your foot back, continuing to follow through by either delivering a second kick to his testicles, or by turning and breaking his leg with a side kick.

As with the side kick, *for street defense use*, no front kick should be aimed above the attacker's groin.

In all, the combined tactics of throwing *anything* directly into the opponent's face and *instantly* following through with continual kicking attacks is the best practical defense against a razor fighter.

THE CHAIR DEFENSE

The old "chair defense strategy" as used by Fairbairn is as good and effective today as it was when he trained OSS and Commando personnel in its use during the 1940's... so long as you've got a chair handy. Pick it up by the back and drive hard into the razor-wielder's advance, jamming the chair's legs into the attacker.

Against a razor (or any other edged weapon attack) a chair can be used with excellent possibility of success. Jab hard, go at him, and be aggressive!

BLOCKS

In a situation where a close, sudden attack against you occurs, about the only thing you can do is use your hands and arms to block any attempt on the antagonist's part to slash you. This is pretty instinctive anyway, and you *must* offer some defense. What you need to keep in mind is that the sooner you convert such an undesirable situation INTO ONE IN WHICH *YOU, YOURSELF* ARE ATTACKING THE RAZOR-FIGHTER, the better!

Once physical contact is made and your block (or attempt to block) has been executed, use your feet and knees against the opponent by delivering scrape kicks down his shinbone or knee kicks into his groin. Be fast! Be ruthless! Unless you throw the razor-fighter on the defensive he will not be deterred from continuing his attack. Just to block or dodge is by no means sufficient.

Defense vs. either *the lapel grab and threat or the razor held at the throat.*

First block aside and grab the weapon hand.

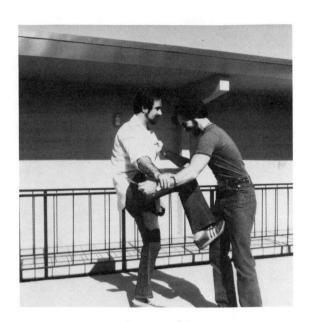

Then, kick groin!

When opponent doubles over, knee face!

NEVER, EVER, EVER, UNDER ANY CIRCUMSTANCES OR CONDITIONS WHATSOEVER attempt to "disarm" the razor fighter by immobilizing his weapon hand and twisting the razor from his grip. A streetwise punk will respond by ramming his fingers in your eyes or biting your throat out. He *won't* respond like you see in the movies by surrendering his weapon.

If your block and kick/stomp response fails to cause him to drop his weapon (as it probably *will* fail) just step back and KICK. Neither attempt to get his weapon away, nor go to the ground with him. Let your strong leg muscles do their job and KICK! Keep kicking and kicking and use your hands only to guard your facial area targets (including your throat). Only if a fortunate opening occurs to rip out your enemy's eyes, rupture his windpipe or crack the bridge of his nose with a bottom-fist or edge-of-the-hand bash, should you substitute a hand blow for your kicks.

Another block. From here a punch into the groin could follow easily. Also, an elbow strike to the solar plexus.

73

Opponent who rushes in with a razor can be blocked as above. Note how the side kick follows perfectly -- ending the fight!

Opponent attempts a downward slash and is parried (similar to punch defense).

74

A knee blow is appropriate as a followup!

SOME PARTING ADVICE ON DEFENSE

Finally, remember to avoid the most serious of all attacks: the surprise attack from behind. Only supreme alertness can help you here, and the common-sense precaution of always having a wall or some other impenetrable object to your back. Luck, the one thing you must never rely on, is insufficient to protect you from a fatally effective surprise attack from behind. So don't hope for luck.

I always tell my pupils: "Never let your guard down. Even if there is no one else on the street with you, stand with your back to the solid barrier of the traffic light when you stop before crossing the street". And that's good advice.

Self-defense is war in microcosm.

LESSON 6: THE RAZOR FIGHT

Razor fighting is not the same as knife fighting -- although experience and training in proper knife fighting methods most definitely has carryover value for razor combat. Primarily, razor fighting is extremely close-in and requires better physical condition than knife fighting, and I think a much stronger stomach. You need, quite literally, to be emotionally unaffected by ripping your opponent to shreds.

In our nation's big cities (such as New York, Chicago, San Francisco, etc.) razor fights occur with regularity largely among rather primitive backward culture types -- usually racial minorities. Those who wish to interpret these words as "racist" are free to do so, but it is not my intention to convey such a meaning. In fact, the poor racial minorities naturally gravitate to less sophisticated and bloodier martial ways. This has always been true, and it is not likely to change. The well-to-do business executive generally either hires a bodyguard (stupid, in my opinion, except in rare cases) or he purchases and learns to use a high quality handgun or shoulder weapon. The ghetto dweller carries a bladed implement or a cheap, practically worthless handgun. There's nothing "racist" in this observation -- it's just plain factual.

Generally speaking, the physical fitness, hardiness and general ruggedness of youthful ghetto punks is extraordinarily high. At an early age they develop a high tolerance for pain and violence, and their combative attitude leaves little wanting. A razor is a logical weapon for such persons.

The average man who wishes to achieve *workable* expertise with a razor -- that will serve in a real fight -- must condition his attitude as well as his muscles to fight ruthlessly and fiercely. Merely mastering some pretty "tricks" won't do at all.

AGGRESSIVENESS AND SURPRISE ARE THE KEYS

You might think that the element of surprise would be impossible to achieve in a face-to-face razor fight, but that isn't necessarily true. While you can't surprise your opponent totally, as you could in a sudden self-defense or offense move, you can surprise him by causing him to believe that you will fight him one way and then furiously attacking in another way.

In the classic text *A BOOK OF 5 RINGS*, the late author Miyamoto Musashi (the greatest swordsman in Japanese history) advises that in personal combat one may achieve victory by commencing in a manner that suggests one will fight slowly, and then suddenly attacking with swift vigor. This is the nature of the surprise that can be achieved in a face-to-face razor fight.

Feigning fear is one of my great fortes. It so beautifully causes one's adversary to plunge ahead, overconfident. Too, it relieves him of qualms about whether or not you represent any threat to him. This makes the bastard grist for your mill! If you can create in your enemy's mind the conviction that you are a pushover, or that you are terrified and cowardly, that's great! Then, at the instant he begins to attack with the certainty that you will be no problem, tear into him screaming like a wild animal and destroy every vital point of his that is open to you. Follow through with obliviousness to your own or to your enemy's injury, and do not stop pounding, ripping and tearing at his carcass until your muscles fail from exhaustion!

Stepping back as though you intended a retreat, and then suddenly charging forward, continuing to follow through, is also good strategy.

Lunging -- then stopping suddenly -- then following through with a final attack that destroys the enemy, often works well.

Deception is everything! Fairness or ethics are laughable.

Obviously, it is important to deceive the adversary whenever possible, and in whatever way is open to one. By implanting -- even momentarily -- an incorrect evaluation of your intentions in your enemy's head, you succeed in totally throwing him off his guard. A man who is genuinely convinced, for instance, that you intend to punch him in the face, is helpless to defend himself against a properly executed, swiftly-delivered kick in the testicles.

Deception is more important than fancy moves. So is attitude.

In a razor fight, the one who wins is always the one who is *determined to win*. This determination reflects itself in two fundamental ways: by aggressive physical and aggressive mental behavior.

No assailant or opponent worth the name will be deterred by your defensively-oriented movements and attitude. If, when embroiled in a fight, you foolishly determine only to defend yourself via non-aggressive or non-offensive actions, you are lost. First of all, no one -- *no matter how great an expert in any form of combat* -- can indefinitely keep up a defensive pose, and endlessly avoid, parry, block, or dodge, or thwart his enemy's advances. Sooner or later he will fail -- and then he will probably be killed. Second, thee can in fact be no successful defense, at any rate, without *some* aggressive, offensive action on your part. Even if you do (wrongly) take a defensive attitude in a fight, and succeed in

77

blocking the enemy, so what? You'll still need to take aggressive action *at some point* to terminate the fight. Unless you neutralize the aggressor you have not defeated him. Better by far to take swift, positive, ruthless and powerful *aggressive action* right away!

Actual combat experience, in military and law enforcement situations (as well as in certain civilian situations) has proven beyond any possible shadow of a doubt that AGGRESSIVENESS and offensively-oriented technique application is the superior approach to dealing with any hand-to-hand adversary(s). In my Basic COMBATO Course (which consists of 20 lessons), it is not unusual for a pupil to achieve enormouse self-assurance and actual, workable close-combat ability by the time he completes his sixth lesson! In fact, I have instances on record where pupils of mine have, with no more than two or three lessons under their belt, actually defeated serious attackers in real-life fight situations and attacks. I do not say this to boast -- I am merely pointing out that stressing *aggressive*, rather than passive (i.e., defensive) skills and attitudes is far and away the superior approach in learning any form of hand-to-hand combat.

The same principle of aggressiveness applies in razor fights, when you have a weapon, as it does in unarmed hand-to-hand when you have only natural weapons with which to fight.

BE AGGRESSIVE!

Let your enemy, in a razor fight, actually perceive that *you are after him!* Your aggressive posture will convey this, and when you *go for him* he will be forced to assume the defensive, which places you instantly in an advantageous and superior position.

PSYCHING OUT THE OPPONENT

Your objective when you attack will always be to convince the enemy that his life is directly in danger. Your posture, attitude, movements, etc. *must cause the enemy to assume that he is facing a wild man*, and a wild man bent upon killing him, to boot!

It matters little if the enemy is your physical superior. Naturally, it is desirable to be bigger and stronger than the enemy, but you are at no psychological disadvantage if this is not the case. In fact, if you are physically inferior to your opponent, *yet take a viciously aggressive, determined and fearless attitude in the fight,* you will most definitely have an advantage. Remember: Your opponent knows clearly that he is bigger than you are, to be sure. If this is so, and if you *still* are fearless and determined to attack him, he will be forced to ask himself what you know that he doesn't!

I do not mean to imply that all the above thoughts will be consciously verbalized inside the enemy's mind during the split-second riposte of hand-to-hand combat; but I do assure you that, for however brief a moment, the enemy's perceptual awareness will be taken up with momentary "concern" over this issue. this, for you, is an incalculable advantage.

You will recall that I said in COMBATO three elements of development are stressed:

Physical Condition

Mental Readiness

Techniques Of Combat

Learning to "psyche out" the enemy is a vital part of the mental readiness training, and you will do well to keep this in mind at all times.

CONVERTING FEAR AND ANGER INTO AGGRESSIVE ACTION

Fear is your greatest ally in a fight. Too bad that many victims of violent crime have let their initial fear response run away with them -- for in actuality that fear *could have saved them from their unfortunate fate, if they had known how to use it!*

What is fear? It is Nature's automatic life-saving mechanism within you that triggers muscle and emotional "readiness" and that starts -- without your conscious decision -- a flow of adrenalin throughout your system that can give you the physical strength to pick up a man twice your size and throw him ten feet. It speeds up you reflexes, sharpens your eyesight and your "sixth sense" and makes you, for the duration, a virtual powerhouse.

Why, you most likely will be asking now, if the above is true, are people defeated by their fear? The answer is that, when fear overtakes them, *they become afraid of their fear,* rather than becoming *aware* of their fear, and channeling its energy. Why does this happen? Because too many of us are too civilized. Over the last hundred years or so we have become so intellectual about our emotions that we tend to *think about them* and *intellectualize about them* much too much, and *we don't act on them when they arise.* Thus, the person who is confronted by a violent aggressor will perceive (properly) that "I am afraid." But then, rather than letting that fear-energy charge him with the power he needs to destroy his foe, he goes on with: "Oh my God! I'm so scared! I may be killed! I'm afraid!" Etc., etc.

This is not cowardice, or in any sense being "yellow", as some rather stupid physical types would have you believe. It is simply the inevitable result of being too civilized!

In actual fact, in order to be successful in the primitive uncivilized arena of hand-to-hand combat, one must forego all "civilized" aspects of his nature. In combat it is most definitely possible to be *too civilized!*

In hand-to-hand combat, if nowhere else, it is to your definite advantage to learn to cultivate the jungle or animal philosophy. You may rest assured that y our opponent will!

Anger is very close to fear, and by cultivating an attitude of *indignant hatred* for violent types you will find that, as your training in combat skills and as your physical capability with techniques improves, you will rapidly go from a fear-response to a fear/anger response when you perceive the possibility of an encounter.

People erroneously believe that anger is a greater impetus to aggressive action than fear. This is *not* true, but because it is a widely-accepted belief, many people tend to convert their anger into action before they convert their fear into action. Actually, in my experience, a person who is terribly afraid *yet who channels that fear into action*, is far more potent than a person who is angry, and who channels the anger into action. Fear touches our own deepest *survival needs.* Anger, too often, is more surface than deep, and it triggers a less desperate response from our mind and muscles.

In any case, and no matter how you choose to look at it, remember that fear and anger can and *must* be used for the energy they provide as strong, primitive emotions, and if you channel the energy provided by fear and/or anger, you can tap a reserve and fount of power that almost guarantees your victory in combat.

SUGGESTIONS FOR WINNING A RAZOR FIGHT

I shall now attempt to give you some combat-proven tips on how to win a razor fight. These are not very pleasant, and I make no apologies for them. They may be necessary to save you, so learn them well.

1. As you close with the opponent fling a handful of dirt, sand, gravel, or any available handy item, into his face. Kick immediately into his knee or shin-bone, and grab his hair with your free hand while you rip his neck with your razor.

80

2. To make a surprise attack on an opponent, suddenly smash your free hand into his face, and jab the closed razor (like a yawara stick) into his groin. As the opponent doubles over from the groin blow, open the razor, and pressing down on the back of his head, open his throat up with a razor attack.

3. As the opponent suddenly attacks you, yell wildly and sidestep his advance, kicking his knee. As you manuever behind him, grab his shoulder or hair and kick to the back of his knee, bringing him down. Rip his throat with a razor slash as he crumples.

4. As an opponent whom you face waves his razor in front of you, front snap-kick at his razor hand (either striking it or missing -- it doesn't matter) and *close in fast* slashing at his eyes with your own blade. A block can be applied as you close in.

5. When an opponent attempts a wide roundhouse type of slash attack, step in and block, and employ a straight-up slash attack, ripping his face completely. Follow through!

Those are suggestions that I now leave you with, hoping they will never be misused. The responsibility of practicing, retaining, and when necessary, applying your skills, is up to you. May you acquire and retain your ability at a high level and may you never have need to use it in earnest.

CONCLUDING REMARKS,
SUGGESTIONS AND ADVICE

In the hands of a skilled, determined combatant, the straight razor is indeed a formidable weapon. However, since the straight razor was never designed with combat per se in mind, it is impossible to make any suggestions on suitable purchase items -- other than broad, general remarks.

I have never seen a sharpened straight razor that was any better or worse than another sharpened straight razor for in-fighting purposes. I could expand this Chapter to 30 pages of nit-picking verbiage, merely to "pad" this book... but I'm certain that serious students of defense would not appreciate this. After all, it *is* true that there are well-made razors and poorly made razors, and even an idiot can grasp that fact. If you go to any decent cutlery shop, the proprietor will be happy to spend an hour discussing the pros and cons of the various razors he's got on hand. Big deal. If you want to collect razors, I refer you to *1000 RAZORS*, by Bill Schroeder, available for $3.95 from Collector Books, PO Box 3009, Paducah, KY 42001. But the various qualities and specifications mean little to the person who's buying his razor to rip a mugger to shreds.

Blade quality probably does matter quite a bit if you want your razor for lifetime use as a shaving implement. Here again, the best information I can give you is to consult the proprietor of a respectable cutlery shop. He knows more about the nitty-gritty of razors for shaving that I even have the interest to hear about.

I would advise the combat-oriented reader of this book to use these simple guidelines in selecting a razor for defense and survival usage:

1. Buy a *new* razor only, unless by dint of experience you can tell there is a flaw in the simple construction of the implement.

2. Avoid spending more than $25 for your razor, unless you are a collector. I have personally visited ten shops in research for this Chapter, and have come to the conclusion that top *practical* quality razors can generally be had anywhere, brand new, for under $25. This does not include ornate designs, but I certainly don't see how a prettily-fashioned handle on your weapon will help you to open a punk's throat any quicker or any better.

3. Buy a razor strop with your blade, since obviously your razor needs to be kept *razor sharp!* If you do use your weapon to sever flesh -- or even clothing -- it will dull the blade. After a thorough cleaning, then, you'll have to sharpen the blade to be sure it's ready for the next encounter. The razor's whole strength lies in its sharp, keen edge. It has absolutely no "heft" to speak of, and no ability to penetrate point-wise with a thrust attack. KEEP YOUR RAZOR SHARP!

4. Spraying your razor *lightly* with WD-40 will keep it in perfect fettle.

5. In my opinion, the best razors are made in either Germany (of Solingen steel) or in England (at Sheffield, where the WWII Commando knives of the Fairbairn-Sykes design are produced). If you think the owner of the cutlery store you go to is full of bananas, check to see that the razor was made in either of the two places mentioned, and you can't get a raw deal.

6. If your razor breaks or chips in combat, get rid of it afterwards and buy a new one. *Don't* rely on a flawed weapon.

7. When purchasing your razor, test it. I don't mean on the salesman, and I don't mean by going through an obvious combat drill while others in the store, awestruck, watch you make an ass out of yourself. I mean hold the razor, see how it feels. Turn to an inconspicuous angle, away from the salesman, and try the grips mentioned in this book. It should take you about two seconds to do this. Try holding the razor (closed) as a yawara stick. *How does it feel?* Only you can answer that question. Some razors have handles that are a bit heftier than others. This can make, for some, a big difference. *Now,* at the time of purchase, is the time to decide what fits you.

I hope that it is obvious, but just in case it isn't, let me point out that only a flaming nincompoop would shoot off his yap about buying the razor for defense. And any "showing off" with your weapon surely makes you a first-class candidate for shithood. Be adult, responsible, quiet and unobrusive about your intentions with your razor. Otherwise you are inviting busybodies, police, do-gooders, and just plain blabbermouths to make your life hell.

Psychologically, the razor is a terrible instrument for use on people. Remember that, *while you may be 100% justified in slicing some young crapbag to ribbons, and leaving him a bloody ripped-up mess in the gutter,* the law may not agree. Especially if the punk was unarmed. I feel that the defender, in any attack situation, is justified in doing -- and in *using* -- any damn thing he wants to or can apply. Why we are obliged to care about creatures that prey upon us is something that I have never been able to understand.

I urge every reader to obey the law. For informational purposes only, I will point out that if your weapon "disappeares" (i.e., is appropriately destroyed and discarded so that it is impossible to retrieve or to ever again find) after use, you *cannot* be proven to be the person who used the weapon on anyone. It is your word against the crapbag's; and since the crapbag probably has a prior record (most violent offenders are today routinely released with a slap on the wrist) your word will out! All of this doesn't apply in your home, naturally. But it does apply in the street. In your home I *hope* you will have access to a 12 guage shotgun or a .45 auto when trouble strikes! At the very least, you should have a fighting knife or a combat-bowie knife in your home.

A WORD TO HUSBANDS AND BOYFRIENDS

Many men, including myself, like the idea of their wives or girlfriends being armed and prepared to eliminate any scum that accosts them. This is prudent, wise and understandable to anyone but a useless, spineless liberal.

I certainly can sympathize with the man who actively encourages his woman to learn martial skills and the proper use of weapons. HOWEVER... please allow me to offer some advice, borne of not inconsiderable experience working with women.

Women tend generally to be very reluctant to use any sort of edged weapon. I have *never* known a female pupil (and I have known many!) who was willing to use a razor against an opponent. It just doesn't suit most women, and frankly I have little question as to why.

Don't try to shame your wife or girlfriend (or bully her) into keeping a razor -- or anything else -- as a weapon, unless she willingly agrees. When the chips are down she will fumble and fail with a weapon she finds abhorent -- and she will probably have it used against her.

A razor-sharp double-edged boot knife (like the Gerber Mark I) is perfect for a woman who will unhesitatingly use it, and who will willingly undergo the ten hours or so of training necessary to insure proficiency. Get your lady a knife, then, if she is agreeable, but not a razor. Not, that is, unless she actually wants one!

84

Ideally, a handgun of .38 caliber or better is the ideal defensive arm for a lady, and she should be encouraged to practice with it until she can pump "2 in the body and 1 in the head in 1½ seconds", as I say to those ladies whom I teach to use handguns.

Razors are not, I'm afraid, for women. Not for any whom I have come into contact with, anyway!

Now our violent little work has come to a close. I sincerely hope that our meeting in these pages has resulted in your attaining greater skill, greater confidence, and greater martial competence than you previously had.

In these violent times, no one can predict if or when you will be the victim of a sudden violent assault. I hope you never are so victimized, but the probability -- so statistics prove -- is always there in presentday America.

Maintain a state of mental and physical preparedness at all times. Learn to use your razor well and carry it when you think you might need it. Never look for trouble, start a fight, or treat another human being in any manner that you yourself would not wish to be treated in.

If trouble strikes, strike back. Hard.

YOU WILL ALSO WANT TO READ:

☐ **34040 SILENCING SENTRIES, *by Oscar Diaz-Cobo.*** The material in this new book is designed to familiarize the reader with the maneuvers that can be used to close in on and remove any enemy sentry. The author holds the rank of 8th Degree Black Belt, and has completed several courses in the arts of close combat. Clear writing and numerous photos make this the best possible book on the subject. *1988, 5½ x 8½, 92 pp, many photos, soft cover. $12.95.*

☐ **19050 SUBWAY SURVIVAL, *by Bradley J. Steiner.*** Written by the author of *Manuals On Mayhem,* and *Close Shaves,* and other well-known self-defense books, focuses his training and knowledge on the problems of self-defense on the subway. If you use mass transit, then this book is for *you. It could just save your life! 1980, 5½ x 8½, 141 pp, profusely illustrated, soft cover. $7.95.*

☐ **934032 PHYSICAL INTERROGATION TECHNIQUES *by Richard W. Krousher*** The book tells you what no other book will: *how to torture information out of an unwilling subject.* Most people will not have the stomach to read it, but those who do will learn more about torture and torment than they dreamed possible. You may not "enjoy" this material, but you'll never forget it! *1985, 5½ x 8½, 93 pp, soft cover. $12.00.*

...And much more! We offer the world's most controversial and unusual books. Please see the catalog announcement on the next page.

————————————————————————CS

LOOMPANICS UNLIMITED
PO Box 1197/Port Townsend, WA 98368

Please send me the books I have checked above. I am enclosing $_____ (which includes $3.00 for shipping and handling).

Name _____

Address _____

City/State/Zip _____

"Yes, there are books about the skills of apocalypse — spying, surveillance, fraud, wiretapping, smuggling, self-defense, lockpicking, gunmanship, eavesdropping, car chasing, civil warfare, surviving jail, and dropping out of sight. Apparently writing books is the way mercenaries bring in spare cash between wars. The books are useful, and it's good the information is freely available (and they definitely inspire interesting dreams), but their advice should be taken with a salt shaker or two and all your wits. A few of these volumes are truly scary. Loompanics is the best of the Libertarian suppliers who carry them. Though full of 'you'll-wish-you'd-read-these-when-it's-too-late' rhetoric, their catalog is genuinely informative."

—THE NEXT WHOLE EARTH CATALOG

THE BEST BOOK CATALOG IN THE WORLD!!!

We offer hard-to-find books on the world's most unusual subjects. Here are a few of the topics covered IN DEPTH in our exciting new catalog:

- *Hiding/concealment of physical objects! A complete section of the best books ever written on hiding things!*

- *Fake ID/Alternate Identities! The most comprehensive selection of books on this little-known subject ever offered for sale! You have to see it to believe it!*

- *Investigative/Undercover methods and techniques! Professional secrets known only to a few, now revealed to you to use! Actual police manuals on shadowing and surveillance!*

- *And much, much more, including Locks and Locksmithing, Self-Defense, Intelligence Increase, Life Extension, Money-Making Opportunities, and more!*

Our book catalog is 8½ x 11, packed with over 500 of the most controversial and unusual books ever printed! You can order every book listed! Periodic supplements to keep you posted on the LATEST titles available!!! Our catalog is free with the order of any book on the previous page — or is $3.00 if ordered by itself.

Our book catalog is truly THE BEST BOOK CATALOG IN THE WORLD! Order yours today — you will be very pleased, we know.

**LOOMPANICS UNLIMITED
PO BOX 1197
PORT TOWNSEND, WA 98368
USA**